As a Christian, it is very important to me to share the love of God every chance I get. As a coach myself, having the opportunity to work with young men is very valuable, especially because you get to have their full attention at times. If you work with young people, I recommend taking the time to read this devotional. I guarantee you will not regret it.

Remember: "As for me and my house, we will serve the LORD" (Joshua 24:15, NKJV).

EDUARDO GONZALES
PASTOR AND SOCCER COACH

Coach Shamberger's devotional is a breath of fresh air in today's challenging sports environment. Michael has a great value for discipleship. I have witnessed the fruit of his influence on many of his players. His insights, challenges, and humor come from real experience and a genuine heart for the reader. This book will be of benefit to players and parents alike.

DAVID SANFORD
NATIONAL DIRECTOR, MISSIONARY ATHLETES INTERNATIONAL

This devotional by K. Michael Shamberger is an awesome reminder of all that is wonderful in sports and can be learned from years of experience. Given his path coaching high school soccer, Michael is able to enlighten and enrich all parents, players, and coaches as to the true meaning of and life lessons achieved through participation in athletics. His devotional is both thought-provoking and joyful. It is an essential read.

MATTHEW (MATT) P. MOELLER
HEAD MEN'S SOCCER COACH, ALBEMARLE HIGH SCHOOL

A great game plan allows for success. My dear friend Michael Shamberger lays out a detailed life game plan, one that teaches us that true winning starts with devotion to God.

STEPHEN TOWNSEND
US ARMY CHAPLAIN

Patience, guidance, understanding, direction, and *love* are words that come to mind as I think about Coach Shamberger on the sidelines of our soccer games while he led our boys through many successful seasons. His care for the team reached far beyond the field, and each individual player knew they were valued. Coach Shamberger was not just a soccer coach to our boys; he was a life coach. This book combines his love of the game, his love for people, and his heart for God into a beautiful collection of devotions. I will forever remain thankful for the way in which he modeled servant leadership and love to our kids on and off the field. No finer coach, mentor, leader, or prayer warrior can be found!

JENNY PURVIS
PRINCIPAL, NORTH MOORE HIGH SCHOOL

Coach Shamberger was one of my coaches when I played soccer at North Moore. Now he has retired, and I am the head coach. Coach Shamberger's devotional is a must read. He provides insights that come from his heart and his wisdom that challenge and excite the reader. His influence on his players throughout his career is reflected by the dedication to his players you read about in this book. This devotional will help everyone's spiritual and athletic life.

LUIS PERALTA
MEN'S SOCCER COACH AND FORMER PLAYER, NORTH MOORE HIGH SCHOOL

Soccer is more than kicking a ball in a net. It is a universal game that brings us together and challenges us to be better people. It's a social lubricant, inviting all people to partner together with one common goal and become more virtuous in the process. In this game, relationships with players, coaches, and fans abound, and opportunities abound for the Christian to become more like Christ and share His love.

As a pastor, soccer player, and coach, I have found this book to be a refreshing outlook on this beautiful game. Rather than being consumed with strategy and technique, Shamberger walks with you daily through the real circumstances of a soccer coach and shows how to manage in a Christlike way. I can only hope more coaches, players, and parents will engage with this book daily and use this sport as a means of growing closer with their team, community, and God.

JARED MCNEILL
PASTOR AND FORMER PLAYER

There are very few people who have had an immediate impact in my life. My good friend, brother in Christ, and life-coaching companion is truly one of those people. "Coach" and I met under a situation that does not typically create a lifelong friend: the soccer field. Let me make it even more delicate and specific. We met as coaching adversaries, representing two different high school boys' soccer teams that were competing for the 2013 1A NCHSAA State Soccer Finals Championship game. The "battle" would rival the greatest of high school games, as it would play through four overtimes and eventually be decided in a sudden-death penalty kick shoot-out. On this particular day, our team would hoist the soccer trophy, yet the ultimate triumph would be one only God would have seen. What I have now come to realize is that day would launch an "inner spiritual battle." That day would unite two opposing coaches from different counties with a common mission to serve the Lord. Coach Shamberger and I share the same passion, which is to mentor our teams and to teach a simple lesson. When you win, you praise God, and when you lose, you praise God. In everything you do, you honor and give God the praise.

Six years later, this book serves as the ultimate trophy for all that pick it up. Immediately, you will see the gift that Coach has for inspiring players, coaches, and families. His coaching philosophies, life lessons, and the Word of God are the immediate impact. I applaud Coach for the vision that God has challenged him with and the lessons we can all take from the soccer field into our homes.

Dr. Michael Graybar, DC
Chiropractic Doctor and Coach

BEYOND THE PITCH

BEYOND THE PITCH

Soccer Strategies for Winning at Life

MICHAEL SHAMBERGER

HiGHERLIFE
PUBLISHING & MARKETING
www.ahigherlife.com

BEYOND THE PITCH: Soccer Strategies for Winning at Life by
K. Michael Shamberger
Published by HigherLife Publishing & Marketing
PO Box 623307
Oveido, FL 32762

Scriptures marked GNT are taken from the Good News Translation
- Second Edition © 1992 by American Bible Society. Used by
permission.

Scripture quotations marked HCSB are been taken from the
Holman Christian Standard Bible®, Copyright © 1999, 2000, 2002,
2003 by Holman Bible Publishers. Used by permission. Holman
Christian Standard Bible®, Holman CSB®, and HCSB® are federally
registered trademarks of Holman Bible Publishers.

Scripture quotations marked NKJV are taken from the New King
James Version®. Copyright© 1982 by Thomas Nelson. Used by
permission.

Scripture quotations marked NIV are taken from the Holy Bible,
new International Version®, NIV®. Copyright© 1973, 1978, 1984,
2011 by Biblica, Inc.™ Used by permission of Zondervan. All rights
reserved worldwide. www.zondervan.com. The "NIV" and "New
International Version" are trademarks registered in the United
States Patent and Trademark Office by Biblica, Inc.™

International Standard Book Number: 9781951492045
19 20 21 22 23 — 987654321
Printed in the United States of America

CONTENTS

Contents

FOREWORD

WHEN I WAS around six years old, my parents and I had discussed the various sports I wanted to play. They gave me the opportunity to try two sports a year. I played basketball and liked it, but most of the kids I played against were better than me. I tried baseball for a while but didn't really enjoy it. Then came soccer. I don't remember much of my first soccer practice, only the instant connection between the ball and my feet. I loved it. My dad remembers what I said as we climbed into our car after that first practice: "Dad, I *love* soccer!"

I could command the ball to go where I wanted it to go, and I somehow naturally understood how to make the game work for me, even though I had never really played it before that day.

Now, fast-forward many years. I graduated from high school with a partial athletic scholarship to play soccer at a Division I program in North Carolina. Thanks to my exposure to and participation in the game of soccer, I have traveled across the globe, playing and coaching the game. I began coaching soccer at various levels, from young children to high-school age, and eventually started my own soccer training company.

During my preteen days, my dad was a truly committed father. He wanted to provide me the opportunity to do something I loved, so he drove me an hour each way to soccer practices twice a week and to multiple soccer games on weekends. After I had my driver's license for a year, my parents allowed me to drive myself to and from practices. They continued, however, to come to all my games when they could.

Soccer gave me many opportunities, not just in sports but in life as well. The connections I made as a player helped me decide which college to attend, find jobs, start a business, and travel around the world, developing relationships with people I would never have met otherwise.

I've seen my dad grow as a person by venturing into coaching soccer too, which was not something he intended to do. I've seen him grow as a coach into somewhat of a local legend in the community. I have seen kids make it a goal to come and play for him because they knew it could very possibly lead to opportunities like going to college. I've seen him mentor young guys from their freshman year in high school into adulthood. I see in my dad that he believes coaching soccer is much more than simply coaching a game. It's a way to impact people's lives, and he lives that out each and every day.

—BENJAMIN SHAMBERGER

ACKNOWLEDGMENTS

THERE ARE WAY too many people to acknowledge and thank for making this book possible, and it would take far too much ink and paper to list every name here. Hopefully, each of you knows your importance to me. However, I do want to acknowledge the following.

My parents, Charlie and Ruth Shamberger: Although gone from this earth and with the Lord now, their influence on my life grows stronger with each passing day. Thank you, Lord, for giving me such wonderful parents!

My dear wife, Dr. Cynthia Thrasher Shamberger: God truly outdid Himself when He gave me Cynthia to be my partner for life. She is such a godly woman of great virtue, strength, and character. Thank you, Cynthia, for sticking with me when neither one of us knew where the solid footing was. I love you more than words can express!

All the soccer players I have coached through the years: Each of you made this book possible, though you did not know it at the time. The secret is that neither did I. Without a doubt, the best part about coaching was the relationships I developed with you. I've had outstanding players through the years who are even better people. Thank you for challenging me and for making me a better coach and a better person. To each one of you who still believes you were my favorite player: You were. I love you guys—and gals!

INTRODUCTION

ONE LOVELY SPRING afternoon, years ago, my son, Benjamin, then a freshman in high school, eagerly greeted me as I arrived home.

"Dad, guess what?" he asked. His excitement was evident, so I knew he had important news to share.

"What, son?"

"The principal said we could have a soccer team this fall at the school!" he gushed. "Isn't this great news?"

"Yes, son. It is wonderful news!"

Then came the bombshell.

"Guess who the coach is going to be?"

Not having a clue, I asked, "Who?"

"You!" he said, without flinching or batting an eye.

"*What?*"

And the rest, as they say, is history.

At the time, we were living in my hometown of Robbins, a beautiful rural village in central North Carolina. There was no soccer of any kind in the local area, not recreational, not school—none. I had moved my family to Robbins about five years earlier from Greensboro, which is where my son began playing soccer, and he loved it. He was also pretty good at it, so when he arrived at North Moore High School and learned there was no soccer team, he and another soccer-loving student lobbied to start one. That fall, the principal turned them down, but in the spring, he gave the okay. He told my son, though, that no one on staff knew anything about coaching soccer. That's when Benjamin volunteered me.

Essentially, I didn't have coaching experience either. I had never played soccer, and to this day, I have not played one single soccer match. And that's true. The only coaching experience I had at the time was coaching my son's recreational team through one six-week season when he was about ten years old.

But in order for my son to have a high school soccer team to play on, I agreed. I accepted the challenge of coaching this new high school soccer team, and I loved it. I wound up coaching the team for nineteen years, and for sixteen of those years, I was the head coach. My North Moore record as head coach was 203 wins, 101 losses and 11 ties. We played in the 2013 North Carolina State Championship game, and twice in the North Carolina State Final Four. We won six conference championships and had a winning record each year that I was the official head coach. I also received several Coach of the Year awards and was an assistant coach in the POWERADE State Games twice.

What I enjoyed most about coaching, far more than teaching the strategies and the x's and o's of the game and learning to handle game management, were the relationships I developed with my players. I learned that the real reason God placed me as a soccer coach was to influence in a positive way the lives of the players I coached. Being successful on the field was icing on the cake.

After retiring at the end of the 2018 season, I felt the need to put together a daily devotional for people who love soccer. I was leery of doing this and held off for several months before finally giving in and sitting down to start writing. The purpose of this soccer devotional is to give Christians who love soccer a resource they identify with that can also help grow their love for Christ and their passion for the game. There is a little something in here for soccer players, coaches, parents, and fans. Even people unaffiliated with soccer will find the principles in the book applicable to their lives. Hopefully, as you read, you'll identify with the stories shared here and will find the Thoughts to Ponder questions thought-provoking and challenging. If you take the time to actually answer the questions, they will lead you to becoming more like Christ, which is the ultimate goal.

So dig in, read, reflect, allow for change, and enjoy.

APPLY YOURSELF

Do nothing out of rivalry or conceit, but in humility con-
sider others as more important than yourselves.
—PHILIPPIANS 2:3, HCSB

Humble yourselves before the Lord, and he will lift you up.
—JAMES 4:10, NIV

WHEN IT COMES to the game of soccer, or sports in general, what does it mean to *apply yourself*? When I think about a player who applies him- or herself, one question that comes to my mind is this: Is this person teachable?

"Coach Shamberger," you might say, "those are two different things," and maybe they are. But you cannot apply yourself if you are not teachable. Being teachable, which means being willing to listen and learn, occurs before you can apply what you have learned. This is true because when you apply yourself, you put what you have learned into practice. This is true for any sport or type of physical or academic training. Being teachable is easier for some people than for others. But all of us need to listen to what others have to say, discern and decide what is good and what is not, then learn from the good and throw out the bad.

When it comes to being part of a team, as a coach I learned early on to listen to my players. You might ask, "Coach, weren't you the leader?" Yes, as coach, I was the leader. But my players were the ones on the field playing the game. They were the ones who experienced the action firsthand. So I learned to listen to what they had to say and to consider their input before making the decision I believed was best for the team. First, I had to learn to apply myself to listening to the players so our team could produce a better outcome on the field.

> When we are teachable, we humble ourselves and show respect and honor to those who teach us.

As a player, you may not always agree with, or even like, your coach or coaches. But you do need to listen to what he or she says, and unless there is just something very wrong with their instruction or advice, you need to apply it in practice and in the game.

When we are teachable, we humble ourselves and show respect and honor to those who teach us. As we apply what we have learned from others, we improve. We also develop character as we apply what we have learned from others by putting it into practice.

THOUGHTS TO PONDER:

- With whom do I need to humble myself?
- Do I need to apologize to anyone?
- What have I learned that I have refused to apply?
- Who can I honor today?

GAME INTEGRITY

Our purpose is to do what is right, not only in the sight
of the Lord, but also in the sight of others.
—2 CORINTHIANS 8:21, GNT

Integrity: the quality of being honest and having strong moral principles.[1]

DURING MY MANY years of coaching high school soccer, I saw the really good, the extremely bad, and the outright ugly of it all. The worst of the worst for me arrived the year the school athletic director asked me to fill in for the girl's head coach, who had an emergency situation. The game I was to coach was in May, close to the end of the season, and this particular game day was very hot. To make matters worse, it was an away game, and only twelve girls could make the trip. One more girl was injured but said if we really needed her, she would try and play, but I said no to that. Right before the start of the game, my assistant checked the weather and told me the local temperature was ninety-four degrees, not including humidity. Like I said, *it was hot and sticky*.

Game time was four thirty in the afternoon. The sun was bright, and not a cloud dotted the sky. Before the game started, I asked the referee if we could add in a water break midway through each half for the safety of the players. He thought it was a good idea but said both team's coaches had to agree. After the referee talked with the other team's coach, he came back and told me that coach would not agree to it. I was stunned. Absolutely amazed. I was also shocked the referee didn't make the call anyway because it was the right thing to do.

---

1 *Lexico*, s.v. "integrity," accessed October 15, 2019, https://www.lexico.com/en /definition/integrity.

As the game went on, one of my players was injured and another was dealing with heat exhaustion. We were playing with nine players against a very talented team, and the girls who were left on the field were tired. Eventually I just quit coaching the game and gave full attention to taking care of my players, even if it meant playing with seven or eight players on the field. Never before or since, have I been so mad as I was at the end of the game that day; all because of the opposing coach's display of unethical behavior, lack of integrity, and poor sportsmanship. (Note: During the second half, he did agree to a water break because his team was winning so badly. This game was played before the nine-goal rule was put in play.)

> We have to keep in mind that a soccer game, a tennis match, a football game, and so on is what it is: a game.

We have to keep in mind that a soccer game, a tennis match, a football game, and so on is what it is: a game. It is not life and death. No one should die playing a sport—period. We must place players' safety first and seriously evaluate whether or not winning a soccer game, or any other sport's game, has taken priority over the value of a human life.

THOUGHTS TO PONDER:

- Do sports play too important of a role in my life?
- Is my identity tied up with my sport?
- Identify changes you need to make in order to make sure sports have the right priority in your life.

PRACTICE INTEGRITY

Whatever you do, work at it with all your heart, as though you were working for the Lord and not for people. Remember that the Lord will give you as a reward what he has kept for his people. For Christ is the real Master you serve.
—COLOSSIANS 3:23–24, GNT

YOU'RE AT PRACTICE. It's a hot, muggy, summer day. Coach just said today is conditioning work. Yeah! Right? Uhhhhhh! The team has eight laps to run. You've run six of them, and everybody is dragging at this point. Other guys on the team say, "Hey, we're tired, and Coach isn't watching. Let's skip the last lap. He won't know." How tempting this is for you. You have the following options: 1) join them and skip a lap, 2) let them skip a lap but keep running until you complete the assigned task, or 3) speak up to your teammates and say, "No, we're a team. Coach told us eight laps, and we're going to run eight laps together as a team. We can do this, guys. Let's go!"

Practice is so very vital to your individual success and to the success of your team. It serves a multitude of purposes: skill building, conditioning, teaching and learning strategies, team camaraderie/ team building, and much more. As a coach, my advice is to utilize practice as a time to take your skills, and thus your game, to the next level. Doing so provides the confidence you need to perform the same way in a game.

Practice is a set-aside time for you to have the freedom to fail again and again while working to get a skill right. Then one day, boom! You do it right, and your confidence just grows! Practice is an investment that, one day down the road, will produce a return you are thrilled with.

If you are a coach, my advice is not to despise practices. Instead, plan for them. Prepare for them. Have an expectant attitude that your players, your team, will take new strides in practice today. Make your practices exciting, challenging, and fun, and your players will step up to your expectations.

Practice is so very vital to your individual success and to the success of your team.

If you are a player, don't dread practices. What do you want to see happen at the end of the season for your team and for yourself? To get there, you've got to put in the work (investment) through both individual training and team practices. So go to practices with a great attitude, and lead your teammates appropriately. See practice as a stepping-stone to get to where you want to get to personally and as a team.

THOUGHTS TO PONDER:

- As a player, what can I do to support my coach at practices? (Remember the story at the beginning of today's devotional?)

- As a coach, how can I make practices more enjoyable yet challenging for my players?

- As either a coach or player, remember that your ultimate boss is the Lord Jesus Christ. Serve Him through how you coach, practice, and play.

INTEGRITY OF PURPOSE
AND MOTIVATION

Whether you eat or drink, or whatever you do, do everything for God's glory.
—1 Corinthians 10:31, HCSB

There's less than a minute to go in the championship game, and the score is tied. The entire game has been a heated, intense battle between two very talented teams. The opposing team was on the attack, but your team just won possession of the ball and is quickly mounting a counterattack. You are on the opposite side of the field from the ball and unmarked. You sprint toward your goal, and sure enough, your teammate crosses you the ball. You receive the pass, beat one oncoming defender, and lift a floater over the keeper's outstretched hands. The ball drops into the upper-ninety back corner of the net. Your teammates mob you while fans scream your praises. You, of course, are ecstatic!

Isn't scoring the winning goal near the end of the game wonderful? Everybody is cheering you on, clapping your back, hugging you, and telling you what a wonderful thing you did. You are basking in the praises you're receiving at that moment.

Celebrations are great, and you should celebrate when wonderful things happen to both yourself and others. Scripture says to rejoice with those who rejoice and to weep with those who weep (Romans 12:15). My question for you, however, is this: What is your motivation for doing what you do? To be an excellent soccer player, parent, or coach requires work, effort, training, and intensity. It requires dedication and diligence to consistently improve to reach the top. What is your "why"? What is your ultimate purpose for playing the game, taking care that your child has what he or she needs to play the game, or coaching a team? Is your motivation self-glory? Or, as a Christian, in your heart and mind, are you asking the Lord that He will somehow be glorified and honored in what you say and do and who you are?

> It's what you work on in private that one day manifests itself in others who desire to be like you.

You see, the glory that comes from winning championships and being a top athlete has its beginnings in the hard work you and others put into making you the best. This happens when no one else is looking. The countless hours and days you put into ball fundamentals, running, sprint work, shooting, and so on will come together one day to make you an excellent player, teammate, and friend. The same can be said for being a role-model parent or coach. It's what you work on in private that one day manifests itself in others who desire to be like you.

The integrity of purpose you privately share with God will reveal itself to those around you. How many times have you prayed and asked God to hold your tongue or help you behave in a manner that shows you are "marked" by Him and are His ambassador? The reason for those prayers is that you might bring Him glory rather than dishonor. Is your purpose God's glory?

THOUGHTS TO PONDER:

- If I were to stand before the Lord today, what would He say about my attitude and behavior as an athlete, parent, or coach?

- What is my ultimate motivation in life, and am I doing a good job of showing that in every area of my life?

- What changes do I need to make in order to glorify God in a more genuine way?

ATTITUDE TOWARD THE COACH

*Do everything without complaining or arguing, so that you may be innocent and pure
as God's perfect children, who live in a world of corrupt and sinful people. You must
shine among them like stars lighting up the sky, as you offer them the message of life.*
—PHILIPPIANS 2:14–16, GNT

THE COACH-PLAYER RELATIONSHIP is powerful and can be a
force for either tremendous good or harm. More than once, I
have heard it said that a coach can be the most powerful influence in a child's life, and I agree with that. A coach is responsible for
teaching, encouraging, motivating, inspiring, giving discipline, challenging, spurring on, and offering even more to their players. If you
are coaching a team sport, you have to make decisions that are best
for the team rather than for individual players, although those decisions affect individual players.

If you are a player, decisions your coach makes for the team may
not always work to your individual advantage. When your coach
has you work on conditioning drills, such as sprints, long-distance
runs, or weight training, they probably don't seem much fun in that
moment. Just the same, at times when the coach corrects you and
tells you to do something differently or when you are disciplined
because you didn't adhere to the team's behavior standards, you
probably don't have fond emotions for your coach. However, he or
she is the coach and the person in authority. You are in a submissive role and are therefore the person who has to respond positively
to the authority. You get to choose your response, and it starts with
your attitude.

Attitude will get you everywhere. A bad attitude will place you on
the bench or even off the team. A great attitude will open doors for

you and promote you over others. The inner motivation and positive attitude you have will push you to excel rather than cheat, to praise and compliment rather than grumble, and to work harder to improve your skills rather than seeing what all you can get away with.

> Attitude will get you everywhere.

THOUGHTS TO PONDER:

- Take some time to examine your heart and attitude. Write or type out your thoughts.

- In what ways can I improve my attitude?

- Think of the attitudes of others around you. Whose attitudes affect you the most (positively and negatively), and why is that?

ATTITUDE TOWARD TEAMMATES

Don't do anything from selfish ambition or from a cheap desire to boast, but be humble toward one another, always considering others better than yourselves. And look out for one another's interests, not just for your own. The attitude you should have is the one that Christ Jesus had: He always had the nature of God, but he did not think that by force he should try to remain equal with God. Instead of this, of his own free will he gave up all he had, and took the nature of a servant. He became like a human being and appeared in human likeness. He was humble and walked the path of obedience all the way to death—his death on the cross. For this reason God raised him to the highest place above and gave him the name that is greater than any other name.

—Philippians 2:3–9, gnt

Teammates. What *are* teammates, anyway? Let's see; these are the ones you work with to accomplish a particular goal. Merriam-Webster's defines a teammate as "a fellow member of a team."[2] When you're on the same team, when all members are working to accomplish the same goal, this means it should be easy to reach that goal, right? Yeah, you know better than that.

Teammates are human beings; they're people. And people are alike in some ways, but in other ways, they are very different. Even people from the same cultural background and the same family can be alike in some ways but quite different in others. The reality is that we tend to focus more on our differences than our similarities, and this can cause problems in teams.

I have coached some very talented teams that did not reach their full potential because personal issues between players adversely affected what happened on the field. I have had teams with lesser

---

2 *Merriam-Webster Online*, s.v. "teammate," accessed October 15, 2019, https://www.merriam-webster.com/dictionary/teammate.

talent outdo themselves because their team chemistry was knit together well; the teammates just clicked, both on and off the field.

> Jesus teaches us in Scripture that we should consider others better than ourselves and seek to help others succeed and prosper (Philippians 2:3–9).

Every coach wants a team of players that get along well with each other, a team without drama issues between players.

For you, as a player, are you a teammate who is easy to get along with? Do you have to have the ball all of the time? Do you have to be the star of the team? Do you look down on teammates who are less talented than you, who come from a lesser socioeconomic background, or whose grades are not as good as yours?

Jesus teaches us in Scripture that we should consider others better than ourselves and seek to help others succeed and prosper (Philippians 2:3–9). How can that possibly work on a team to your advantage? Here's something I've told my players for many years: When each player improves individually, we get better as a team. The better we each are, the more successful we become together. The reality is, the more you help others, the more likely you are to reach your goals.

THOUGHTS TO PONDER:

- Do I look down on anyone on my team for any reason? (Don't be too quick to answer this question. If you find that the answer is yes, pray a prayer of repentance to God, and ask Him to change your heart. You may need to ask forgiveness of the other player as well.)

- In what ways can I work to improve my team?

- Going forward, if you encounter teammates who are not getting along, instead of stirring dissension, challenge yourself to be a peacemaker and an agent of reconciliation.

ATTITUDE TOWARD REFEREES

"Blessed are the merciful, for they will be shown mercy."
—MATTHEW 5:7, NIV

We are therefore Christ's ambassadors, as though God were making his appeal through us. We implore you on Christ's behalf: Be reconciled to God.
—2 CORINTHIANS 5:20, NIV

I HAVE NEVER WANTED to be a referee—not ever. In my opinion, it takes a special quality of person to be a referee. If a referee's call makes one team happy, the other team is upset about it. And if the situation is reversed later in the game, then the once-happy team is upset and everybody is unhappy. Not only are players and coaches bothered; the fans are ticked off with the referee too. So a referee has to be thick-skinned to be able to call the game as he or she sees it with integrity.

When my two children participated in sports when they were younger, I watched how coaches and parents, in particular, reacted to a referee's call during games. It was obvious some parents were living out their own dreams through their children's successes or failures. These parents' angry reactions completely overshadowed the real reason children should participate in sports: to play a sport they enjoy, get exercise, and learn to get along and share with others. Often parents' reactions toward referees were totally out of balance when held against the true purpose of playing sports.

Referees are there to ensure fairness in the game, that the rules are adhered to, and that players are as safe as possible. We, as players, coaches, parents, and fans, need to keep proper perspective regarding officials. Referees are people, and it's guaranteed that they will make mistakes from time to time, just like we do in our daily lives. We need to grant them mercy, and when we do want to protest, we need to do so in a respectful way. There is a right way and a wrong way to do things. There is also a matter of timing. Saying or doing something in the heat of the moment, when you are emotional, may cause you to react in a way you will regret (or should regret) later. Remember that Christ goes with you everywhere you go, and you are His representative at all times and places.

> Referees are there to ensure fairness in the game, that the rules are adhered to, and that players are as safe as possible.

THOUGHTS TO PONDER:

- When I see referees before or during a game, do I automatically have negative thoughts toward them? Why is that?

- What needs to change in my thoughts and actions toward referees?

- In what specific ways can I show more mercy toward referees?

- When I want to protest a referee's decision, what would be the appropriate way to do so as a representative of Christ?

ATTITUDE TOWARD OPPOSING PLAYERS

"So in everything, do to others what you would have them do to you."
—MATTHEW 7:12, NIV

ONE OF THE best things about sports, in my opinion, is the respect you can have for opposing players. This may sound strange to you, but I will explain. Throughout my nineteen years coaching high school boys' soccer, two teams stand out to me still.

One team was one we played several times in the first five to eight years of our program's existence. That team was Jordan-Matthews from Siler City. They won a state championship (maybe more than one), always had very talented players, and had a high-quality coach, Paul Cuadros. I mention them because we always lost to them, except the last time we played them.

Jordan-Matthews was in our conference for a time, so we played them twice during the regular season, and too many times we were matched against them in the early rounds of the state playoffs. Neither team wanted to see the other one so early in the playoffs. (Why the state selection committee did that, I will never know.) Even though we lost to them each time we played them, my players and I knew they would challenge us and make us better. The last time we played them, we beat them, and that's when I knew our program had genuinely arrived as a quality soccer program.

The other team that stands out to me still today is Wallace-Rose Hill. We only played them twice, but both were amazing games. The first time we played them was in the state championship game of 2013. The second time was early in the following season, in the Kick-Off

Classic game. We lost to them both times. The state championship game went to four overtimes and penalty kicks. The second game was a tied game until, with just a few minutes left in the game, they scored to win by one goal. Both games were intense, high-quality, highly competitive games. They were games others who know soccer well described to me as "classics." Like Jordan-Matthews's players from years earlier, Wallace-Rose Hill's players were extremely talented with no weaknesses on the field at all. Their coach, Michael Graybar, was knowledgeable and cared deeply about his players. When our teams played each other, both teams' skills improved. We made each other better. Both teams had a deep respect for the other.

> When playing against either a highly skilled or a lesser-skilled team, respect your opponent.

When playing against either a highly skilled or a lesser-skilled team, respect your opponent. Each person on the opposing team is created by God and has the exact same value as you and your teammates. Yes, you want to beat them in the game, but in doing so, have respect for them as a fellow human being placed here on this earth. Don't call them disrespectful names, talk bad about them, spit on them, or intentionally trip or kick them. That's not how God wants to be represented, and it's not how you improve.

THOUGHTS TO PONDER:

- Although an opposing player may be more skilled than you, discern what can you learn from him or her that will benefit you.

- What do I need to change in my thinking and action toward opposing players?

RESPECT THE OPPOSING COACH

Whenever you possibly can, do good to those who need it.
—PROVERBS 3:27, GNT

S O THIS GUY across the field is your opposing coach. He has brought his team to crush your team. The natural reaction of your flesh (carnal nature) is not to think kindly of this person and to disrespect him. As a matter of fact, you want your team to crush his team. In order for that to happen, you have to hate the guy, right? Absolutely not.

Everyone might not think this way, but my experience has taught me that, for the most part, the best-quality teams my teams faced were coached by some of the highest-quality people—people I grew to respect and wanted to learn from. In my early coaching years, when I knew nothing about what I was doing, one of the best things I did was carefully observe other coaches. I watched what they did, how they handled their players, and how they acted and reacted in different situations. I learned a lot just by doing this. The next thing I did was talk with other coaches, ask questions, and listen. Without fail, the majority of information I was given had to do with building connections with the players and a little bit about the strategies of the game of soccer. This helped confirm the direction I was already moving in my coaching career.

In the previous devotional, I mentioned coach Paul Cuadros. Again, here was a quality coach with an outstanding team. For two years in a row, we played his team on our Senior Night game. Our tradition was to honor our seniors after the end of the game. Each year, I wrote something up about each senior for the announcer to read, and I gave them each a meaningful gift. When Paul heard over

17

the loud speaker that we were honoring our seniors after the game, he asked me during the postgame handshake if he could bring his team over to our sideline and watch our senior presentation. He and his team stayed for the entire event—both years—and we brought both teams together for pictures after the ceremony.

> It showed the players and fans of both schools that you don't have to be enemies to be highly competitive against each other on the field but friends off of it.

That's what I call class. It showed the players and fans of both schools that you don't have to be enemies to be highly competitive against each other on the field but friends off of it. Also, when we went to the state championship game, Paul came to cheer us on, and I went to support him and his team the year they won it.

As a coach, remember that the man or woman leading the opposing team is in the same position you are. He or she is carrying great responsibility, trying to motivate, teach, challenge, and inspire, all while teaching life lessons through sports.

THOUGHTS TO PONDER:

- What are some things I can learn from people I coach against?
- Instead of pulling against opposing coaches, what are some ways I can work to support and encourage them in order to make the game and the experience better for all?

EXHIBIT HOSPITALITY
WHEN HOSTING

"So in everything, do to others what you would have them do to you."
—MATTHEW 7:12, NIV

Offer hospitality to one another without grumbling.
—1 PETER 4:9, NIV

IT'S SATURDAY MORNING. Normally you would be taking it easy, eating a late breakfast, lounging around, and enjoying some java. Things are a little different this morning because you and your wife are hosting dinner guests tonight, and the house is not presentable. So instead of chillin' out, you and your wife are busy cleaning the house inside and out and putting special touches in place to welcome your guests and to make them feel comfortable in your home.

Contrast that with what happens when you are the home-team coach and the visiting team is preparing to arrive. If you are fortunate enough to have locker rooms for the visitors to use, what shape is that room in? Have the bathrooms been cleaned? Is there junk all over the floor from the last team that was in there? Do you welcome them when they arrive? Is water provided for them?

Before you ask if I provided all of these things for each of my home games, the answer is definitely not. But I did try. What I'm getting at

> Being hospitable is just the neighborly thing to do.

is, what is your attitude, and what is your effort? When it comes to being a high school soccer coach, you can feel like you are left to handle everything yourself when it comes to hosting and game-day preparation, depending on the level of support you get from your athletic director and school administration. I liked to welcome the other team and coach shortly after their arrival in order to inform them where the restrooms were, to let them know the pregame routine, and to ask if he or she had any questions. This did not always work out because there were so many tasks to take care of and responsibilities to handle for home games; sometimes I would not be available when the opposing team arrived. But I would do it as soon as I could get around to it.

Again, what is your attitude, and what is your effort? Being hospitable is just the neighborly thing to do. It shows respect and consideration for the other team, and it's doing unto others as you would have them do unto you.

Thoughts to ponder:

- What has been my attitude toward hosting opposing teams?

- What could I do to welcome the visiting team?

KEEP COOL IN HEATED MOMENTS

If you become angry, do not let your anger lead you
into sin, and do not stay angry all day.
—Ephesians 4:26, GNT

WHETHER YOU ARE a soccer player, coach, parent, or fan of the game, heated moments come with the territory. Hopefully there's not a heated moment in every game, but in some games, there generally are.

Here's an example. One of your defensemen is marking an opposing player in the box. The two players collide, and the referee calls a penalty kick. From your perspective, it is a horrible call because it was an innocent entanglement of the feet. Then several more calls are made that also unfairly favor the other team. Your temperature is rising. Your blood pressure is going up fast. You take a deep breath and say, "Okay, Lord, I need You to help me." Before you can finish saying that quick prayer, one of your players is cleated and no call is made. Your player is lying on the field, screaming in pain, and the referee has not even stopped the game for your player's injury. You are about to lose it and run onto the field without permission to check on your player. You scream at the referee, but what is it that comes out of your mouth at that moment?

Are you a representative of Christ in this moment, or have you laid your Christianity aside for just a little bit? Remember that we can never lay our Christianity aside, even in the heat of the moment. When Jesus was on the cross in severe pain, blood pouring out of His body, thirsty, and feeling neglected, He didn't quit or remove Himself from the cross. He endured. He went through the situation, successfully completing his mission on earth.

For us, yes, there are definitely times when we need to stand up for our players or our team. The question is, How do we do it? There was one year that my team was in a playoff game and we were playing away from our home field. The game was being called in an extremely one-sided manner. My players were being kicked, punched, and stepped on intentionally, and nothing was being called. I was protesting to the referees but to no avail. One player after another came off the field hurt; it got so bad that I eventually left the sidelines and stepped several yards onto the playing field in order to get the referee to stop the game. When he did, I called him over to me and told him in few deliberate words that if this continued, I would pull my team off the field and report him and his crew to the state association. After that, he finally started making some calls going our way.

> You take a deep breath and say, "Okay, Lord, I need You to help me."

Did I handle it in a Christlike manner? I believe so. I did not cuss. I didn't even yell or scream. I just looked him straight in the eye and, with all sincerity of voice, tone, and words, told him what I thought and what the ramifications would be if things continued as they had been going. As coach, I needed to defend my players, but I knew I had to act in a respectful manner.

THOUGHTS TO PONDER:

- Reflect back on some heated moments you've been in. How did you handle yourself and others? Was your reaction God-pleasing?

- What can you do now to prepare yourself mentally and spiritually for your next heated moment?

VALUE PLAYERS AS PEOPLE FIRST

Instead, be kind and tender-hearted to one another, and for-
give one another, as God has forgiven you through Christ.
—EPHESIANS 4:32, GNT

Therefore encourage one another and build each other up, just as in fact you are doing.
—1 THESSALONIANS 5:11, NIV

HERE IS YOUR ten-million-dollar question: What is the danger of playing for a coach whose personal identity is rooted in the success of his or her team? Think about this until you come to an answer.

Consider this: The Jaguars and the Dawgs are playing for the conference championship at the end of the regular season. It has been a thrilling game, and the score is tied at 2–2 with less than a minute to go. The Jaguars are on the attack, and the Dawgs' center back, who is an outstanding player, goes to clear a high-arcing ball being crossed in. Just as he is heading the ball to clear it, the keeper decides that he can catch it and races out toward the ball without calling for it. The header is mis-hit and goes over the outreached hands of the goalie and into the net for an own goal. The Jaguars win the game.

After the game, the Dawgs' center back and goalkeeper are just crushed at the mistake they both made and are bawling in tears on the sidelines. Some of the players are trying to console them. The coach for the Dawgs walks over to them and in anger and disappointment says, "You two guys are the sorriest excuse for soccer players I have ever seen in my life. You should feel horrible, and I hope this feeling stays with you for a very long time. You just cost our team the championship." Then the coach storms off mad.

Did you get an answer to that question I asked you above? Something like the scenario I just described to you could be the answer. And if you think that description is unreal, think again.

The young people we coach are gifts that are loaned to our influence for a short period of time. We need to self-evaluate to make sure we are not only using them to advance our own career, fame, and financial opportunities. As coaches, we can build players up or tear them down. It's our job to build them up. It's our job to use soccer to teach them about life. Such things as responsibility, endurance, perseverance, sharing, helping others, working for a common goal for the betterment of all, integrity, family, and more are all part of coaching. Teaching the strategies and skills of the game are just highways with many exit ramps for teachable moments. When your players leave your tutelage, hopefully they carry with them valuable life lessons you have taught them and will remember you in a positive light many years later because they felt loved and valued by you.

> The young people we coach are gifts that are loaned to our influence for a short period of time.

Thoughts to ponder:

- How can I better show my players I value them as people first?

- What are some life lessons I teach now or can begin to teach my players?

- What will my players say about me twenty years from now?

HELP PLAYERS IN ROUGH SITUATIONS

I know that the Lord secures justice for the poor and upholds the cause of the needy.
—Psalm 140:12, niv

*Make certain you do not perform your religious duties in public
so that people will see what you do. If you do these things publicly, you will not have any reward from your Father in heaven.*

*"So when you give something to a needy person, do not make a big show of
it, as the hypocrites do in the houses of worship and on the streets. They do
it so that people will praise them. I assure you, they have already been paid
in full. But when you help a needy person, do it in such a way that even
your closest friend will not know about it. Then it will be a private matter.
And your Father, who sees what you do in private, will reward you."*
—Matthew 6:1–4, gnt

DURING MY COACHING career, I had the honor and privilege of helping some of my players and their families who were in difficult situations. Of course, I did not go public with these events, as it would have embarrassed the players and their families. These circumstances ranged from economic difficulties to family issues to legal problems and more.

One common element among all the players and families I was blessed to help was that none of them wanted their troubles known to others. Although the athlete tried hard to not let it show, sometimes his soccer game suffered and he was not very social with his teammates. These were signs to me that something was wrong. And usually I was right.

Our players are people, and people have problems. How you handle your athlete in that moment will impact him and his family for many years to come, either positively or negatively. But you might say to me, "Coach, that's not what I'm here for. I only signed up to coach soccer." My response to you would be, "It comes with the territory." When you see a player who continuously looks downcast or is significantly off his or her game, that's when you need to privately ask him or her what is going on. You might not be the specific answer they need, but you might be able to point that person to the answer or direct him or her to resources that can help. And please remember that unless it is something you are required by law or by ethics to report, please keep it confidential. Respect their privacy and their dignity.

> How you handle your athlete in that moment will impact him and his family for many years to come, either positively or negatively.

THOUGHTS TO PONDER:

- If I was in a difficult situation, such as a homeless or broken family, how would I want to be treated?

- The devotional mentioned some signs players might display when in a difficult situation. What other signs might you need to be attentive to?

- Why is it important to meet the needs of others when I have it in my power to do so? (Hint: Proverbs 3:27–28.)

RESPECT THE OPPOSING TEAM'S PROPERTY

"Do to others what you would have them do to you."
—MATTHEW 7:12, NIV

Scenario #1

Your team's bus arrives at the opposing team's home facility. You tell your players to disembark and to go use the restrooms first. When you enter the restroom, you notice there is some paper on the floor and that the sinks and commodes are not as clean as you would like. However, when all the members of your team have finished using the facility, you take a final look and see there is much more paper on the floor than before your team went in there. You call your team together and tell them that although the floor had some paper on it when you arrived, they are going to go back in there and pick up all the paper on the floor before going onto the field.

Scenario #2

Both teams are on the field, going through their pregame warm-up. You, as the coach, are standing on the sidelines, watching your team and getting a feel for their mental preparedness for today's game. Just then, a ball from the home team slowly rolls into your team's end of the field. One of your players notices it and gathers the ball. He sees the markings are different from the markings of your team's balls, but instead of sending it to the home team's end of the field, he keeps it and begins using it. What do you do, and what do you say to your player?

The Scouts have a slogan that goes something like "Leave it better than you found it." In the first scenario, it would be very easy to notice the paper that was on the floor when you entered the restroom and to take on the mentality of, "It's okay for us to trash the place, since it wasn't clean when we got here." You don't know who it was that put that trash there before you or why the sinks and commodes had not been cleaned. Plus, by leaving the restroom cleaner than you found it, that's going to be a blessing to somebody.

> What you hold your players accountable for also sends messages to them that they will remember for a long time.

In relation to both scenes, the process of sports is full of teachable moments. These can be valuable for life learning and practical application. What you allow your players to get away with sends unspoken messages to them. What you hold your players accountable for also sends messages to them that they will remember for a long time. By not allowing your player to keep that ball, you are sending a message that it is not okay to steal or take what is not yours. That same message may be remembered by that player months or years later and keep him or her out of jail or prison. As a coach and as a parent, you are constantly teaching, whether you intend to or not.

THOUGHTS TO PONDER:

- Think about the life lessons you are teaching your players. Write those out.

- In what ways can I implement "Do to others what you would have them do to you"?

SPORTSMANSHIP

In all things you yourself must be an example of good behavior.
—Titus 2:7, GNT

"But now I tell you: love your enemies."
—Matthew 5:44, GNT

*Sportsmanship: ethical, appropriate, polite and fair behavior
while participating in a game or athletic event.*[3]

S PORTSMANSHIP IS EMPHASIZED more by some schools, coaches, and referees and less by others. I am a strong believer in it. Sportsmanship shows respect, and I believe each person deserves to be shown respect and treated in a way that shows their value and human dignity. Unfortunately, that same belief is not always expressed in return.

I cannot tell you the number of times that after the handshake at the end of the game, my players would tell me that a player from the opposing team did not shake hands, said something inappropriate, or spit on his hands before shaking my guys' hands. Whenever this happened, if we were still at the field, I would go speak with the other coach about what happened. I wanted him to know what my guys had told me, and it was then left up to him to handle his player. And yes, there were a few occasions when an opposing coach would do the same with me regarding one of my players. My guys knew I didn't put up with disrespecting others and that they would have punishment at practice if these things happened.

---

3 *Your Dictionary Online*, s.v. "sportsmanship," accessed October 15, 2019, https://www.yourdictionary.com/sportsmanship.

But, of course, good sportsmanship is not just giving the obligatory handshake before or after a game. Good sportsmanship is also identified by the way you play and the way you win and lose. There are appropriate and inappropriate ways for each. In my first two years of coaching, we lost more games than we won, and sometimes my players would get frustrated and upset. I had to teach them my values and expectations for their behavior, win or lose. I had to remind them more than once that even though they had all this passion for the game of soccer, it was just that—a game. We needed to put it in perspective and learn life lessons from this beautiful game. In my remaining years of coaching, we won way more games than we lost, and I had to teach my players about winning gracefully and with class. It was important to me that we never looked down on an opponent or treated someone as "less than." We ourselves knew all too well what that felt like.

> Sportsmanship shows respect, and I believe each person deserves to be shown respect and treated in a way that shows their value and human dignity.

You may be tired of hearing me say it, but I feel like I cannot emphasize enough that as Christians we are always, in all times and all places, representatives of Jesus Christ, including on the soccer field. We must take on that mentality and live our lives accordingly.

Thoughts to ponder:

- How do I see sportsmanship?
- What value does sportsmanship hold for me and my team?
- As I value others and behave as a representative of Christ at all times, how does this affect my behavior toward others?

IS YOUR IDENTITY IN SOCCER OR CHRIST?

"Worship no god but me."
—Exodus 20:3, GNT

*"'These people, says God, honor me with their words, but their heart is
really far away from me. It is no use for them to worship me, because
they teach human rules as though they were my laws!'"*
—Matthew 15:8–9, GNT

WE AS HUMAN beings identify with (mentally or emotionally attach ourselves to) lots of things and people. We identify with our family, our city, our ethnicity, our job, our favorite sports teams, and the list goes on. To an extent, there is nothing at all wrong with that. We are from a certain place. We are part of a certain group, and we should connect with that. However, when I ask the question, "Is your identity in soccer?" I am talking about the extent to which you and others are harmed by that. You might ask, "How can I be harmed by having my identity in soccer? It's a healthy, wholesome game."

Have you ever seen a soccer player who lived, breathed, and slept soccer? Seriously. There is something about the game of soccer that can be very addictive and causes fans to be extremely passionate about their favorite team and player. Have you heard of fans stampeding and getting killed in soccer stadiums around the world because of their extreme passion for the game? They place their whole identity in the success or failure of that team or player. If their team wins, they are going to have a really glorious day or night. If their team loses, gloom and despair stay with them for a long time, adversely affecting their relationships, job performance, and other matters.

When our identity (self-worth, value, esteem) is in anything other than Christ, we rise and fall with the instability of what we have placed our confidence in. If our team loses an important game, we are knocked out of our correct place of functioning. We are upset with family members when they have done nothing against us. We can't perform our best work on the job or at school because we can't focus on the work at hand. We lose sleep at night because we are just sick about what happened to our team.

> If our identity is in Christ first, we will not be devastated when our team loses or our favorite player gets injured or plays poorly.

It is of utmost importance that if we find ourselves in a scenario of similar description, we repent to God for misplaced identity and place our identity fully and foremost in Jesus Christ. Remember, in true repentance we turn from one thing and turn to another. We need to be Christians first who happen also to love and appreciate the game of soccer, rather than soccer aficionados who happen also to be Christians.

If our identity is in Christ first, we will not be devastated when our team loses or our favorite player gets injured or plays poorly. We will be able to put a correct perspective on the situation and see that this is simply a recreational pursuit that we get to enjoy along with many others. It is not an essential element of life and will not determine our eternal destiny. This is only a game we get to enjoy. My worship and my greatest passion goes to the almighty God, who created me and called me into existence and for whom I live.

THOUGHTS TO PONDER:

- Ask yourself, "What am I worshipping (praising, exalting, esteeming, being devoted to)?" Take some time to honestly determine your answer and write out your thoughts.

- In thinking about priorities in your life, is soccer too high a priority on the list? If so, determine what needs to happen to correct that.

- In looking at what you say you value versus what your life reflects that you value, who is being harmed, and what do you need to do about it?

PARENTS: DO NOT LIVE YOUR LIFE THROUGH YOUR CHILD

You see, at just the right time, when we were still powerless, Christ died for the ungodly. Very rarely will anyone die for a righteous person, though for a good person someone might possibly dare to die. But God demonstrates his own love for us in this: While we were still sinners, Christ died for us.
—ROMANS 5:6–8, NIV

Love is patient, love is kind. It does not envy, it does not boast, it is not proud. It does not dishonor others, it is not self-seeking, it is not easily angered, it keeps no record of wrongs. Love does not delight in evil but rejoices with the truth. It always protects, always trusts, always hopes, always perseveres.
—1 CORINTHIANS 13:4–7, NIV

YOU ARE AT the soccer field an hour early because your daughter's team needs to go through the warm-up routine before the game. There is a game going on in front of you, so you decide, "Hey, I may as well go and watch that game and kill some time." The first thing you notice is what I will call "aggressive parents." These parents are not simply cheering for their team; they are yelling and screaming at their own children and the referees on the field, and they are complaining openly about their team's coach. You're asking yourself, *Is that the way I am when my child is playing?* Just then, a goal is scored against this team, and you hear a loud yell from whom you assume to be the goalie's dad: "Didn't I tell you to come out to decrease her angle? You can't just stand there like a knot on a log!" You are crushed, and you know the goalie is. You can see it on her face and in her body language.

Scenes similar to this are far too common in sports today. What's driving this? It could be a number of things, but my guess is a prominent reason is that some parents are trying to live vicariously through their children. These parents seek their own success through the success of their children. The more successful their children are, the better they look as parents.

There is a great danger to this situation. If a child feels that he or she has to perform to win the acceptance and love of the parent or parents, the constant pressure to reach perfection will create an unstable parent-child relationship. Our heavenly Father loves us unconditionally. It is very true that He doesn't like our sin, but His love for us as a person never changes or wavers.

> If a child feels that he or she has to perform to win the acceptance and love of the parent or parents, the constant pressure to reach perfection will create an unstable parent-child relationship.

THOUGHTS TO PONDER:

- How am I treating my son or daughter when he or she disappoints me?

- An apology from you may be in order. If so, give a heartfelt genuine apology at the right time and place.

- Pray and ask God to convict you by way of the Holy Spirit any time you are getting out of line.

ACT WITH GODLY CHARACTER

"But I say to you, love your enemies, bless those who curse you, do good to those who hate you, and pray for those who spitefully use you and persecute you."
—MATTHEW 5:44, NKJV

N O MATTER WHAT level of soccer you coach, there is someone who is over you, a leader you report to. The administration over you can be a great benefit and blessing to you or a tremendous frustration. Hopefully for you it is a benefit, but I have met many soccer coaches who felt quite alone and abandoned by their leadership over them. This is not unique to soccer. It happens in careers across the spectrum.

For those who coach high school soccer in America, I have found it to be especially difficult to feel properly supported and funded if your school considers itself to be a football school first. For coaches who find themselves in this situation, it is not uncommon to find favor and resources going to football, basketball, and baseball (the traditional American sports) that do not come to soccer. This can be expressed in a number of ways.

Here is one example. I took my team to an away conference game. The home school definitely had a football-first mentality. When we arrived, the school's football team was on the stadium field practicing, and it was not a game day for them. Well-known customary practice in our area is for the field to be available for use by the two soccer teams at least one hour before the scheduled game time. Since the football team was on the field and it was within that one-hour time frame, I went and spoke with the home-team soccer coach to ask what was going on. The aggravation and annoyance on the coach's face and in his voice were obvious. I was told the football team was not supposed to be on the stadium field at all and that the football coach knew there was a scheduled soccer game that day. I then went to one of the assistant football coaches to ask what time they were going to leave the field. He looked at me, obviously perturbed, as if to ask, "Why are you even breathing?" He basically avoided answering my question, so I walked back to my team's side of the field and told them to take the field anywhere there was open space. We did. The football team left the field about ten minutes after we went onto the field, which was about twenty minutes later than they should have left.

> Love your enemies, and by doing so, maybe your conduct will win them to Christ one day.

This situation should have never occurred, but scenes similar to this happen far too often when coaches of certain sports know they can get away with stuff that would not be tolerated if the situation were reversed. A supportive and fair administration would have been very helpful in that circumstance.

My point in sharing this is that whether you have a supportive administration over you or not, you should act in a way that reveals godly character. Pray for those who do wrong to you. Love your enemies, and by doing so, maybe your conduct will win them to Christ one day. If you do this sincerely and consistently, they will notice that something is different about you. Then you can share the gospel message with them when they ask.

THOUGHTS TO PONDER:

- How do I generally react when I have to deal with difficult people?

- What prayers am I praying for the leadership over me? (See 1 Timothy 2:1–4.)

GIVE THANKS AND SHOW APPRECIATION

Give thanks to the LORD, for he is good; his love endures forever.
—1 CHRONICLES 16:34, NIV

WHILE YOU ARE hard at work during soccer season, you probably do not give a whole lot of thought toward showing appreciation. If you're a coach, you're focused on planning for practices, thinking on game strategies, developing players, and preparing for games, along with other responsibilities. If you're a player, you're focused on what you did during the last game that was either outstanding or stunk the place up. You want to know how you can get better. You are trying to stay healthy or get healthy again. And if you are a parent, you're concerned with schedules and equipment and the other needs of your player.

We have special occasions, such as at the end of the soccer season, when we thank people, and we have the Thanksgiving holiday, when we generally take time to appreciate God and others. But being grateful should be an everyday way of life for all of us. Being thankful keeps us humble because we realize it's not all about us. Taking time to stop and reflect upon the many, many blessings we have will cause a heart of appreciation to spring forth from within us.

If you are a soccer player, simply being able to run up and down a field is more than enough to be grateful for. There are many people on this earth who are afflicted with diseases and physical ailments who cannot run. The fact that you get to play a game (which is an option or a luxury) when many children around the world are dodging bullets and bombs is humbling. Many of these same children are extremely thankful on the rare occasions when clean water is provided to drink and basic food is available to eat.

If you are a coach, you have been entrusted with the privilege of motivating and inspiring those under your tutelage. You are a leader, and you have been tasked with influencing others in a right way. Be thankful for that opportunity.

> If you are a coach, you have been entrusted with the privilege of motivating and inspiring those under your tutelage.

If you are a parent, you get to see memories made over and over. Put them in your memory bank. You will be glad to have them years from now. You also have the opportunity to watch your daughter or son grow and develop both as a person and as an athlete. Additionally, you have someone (the coach) who is assisting you in helping to teach and influence your child in an appropriate way.

These are just a very few examples of what you can be thankful for. Now, go out and show your appreciation to the right people. Don't wait till the end of the season or Thanksgiving to do it. Tomorrow is not promised. For that matter, neither is the rest of today. Be thankful.

Remember this: when you genuinely show appreciation to someone, it brightens their day and our heavenly Father is pleased.

THOUGHTS TO PONDER:

- For starters, list out ten things you are thankful for.

- What are some ways I can show appreciation more often?

- Why do I think God wants us to have an attitude of gratefulness?

ALL PLAYERS ARE
ESSENTIAL TO THE TEAM

Rejoice with those who rejoice; mourn with those who mourn.
—ROMANS 12:15, NIV

T EAM. WHAT COMES to mind when you see or hear this word? Here are two definitions found in Google's online dictionary for the word *team*: "a group of players forming one side in a competitive game or sport" (noun) and "come together as a team to achieve a common goal" (verb).[4]

In these definitions, the words *group*, *one side*, *come together*, and *achieve a common goal* stand out to me. I see a picture of togetherness, unity, and oneness in these words.

On your soccer team, you have a group of athletes who are different from each other, but they share a common goal. Their hairstyles may be different. Their skin tones may be different. Their talent levels may be different. But they all want to go undefeated and win the championship.

Each day in practice, the least talented guys work just as hard, if not harder, than the star players.

They endure the long-distance run. They suffer through the sprint work. They participate in the exercises and drill work. They work hard in practice to make your best players better. But it's the star players who get the recognition. So, one of the values I have tried to emphasize through the years is finding ways to give some recognition to each player.

---

4 *Online Google Dictionary.* s.v. "team," accessed October 15, 2019, http://googledictionary.freecollocation.com/meaning?word=team. .

One example of this was having the game announcer call out the names of all of my players during the pregame player introductions. When I first started doing this, I noticed how the nonstarters' faces lit up with pride when their names were being called and they ran out to midfield along with the starters. For most of the nonstarters, this was the only time they got to be in the

> On your soccer team, you have a group of athletes who are different from each other, but they share a common goal.

spotlight. Having their parents, family, and friends at the game to hear their name called and see them standing at midfield was affirmation of their position on the team and their hard work. It was a proud moment they worked hard for in practice, even if they weren't the most skillful players on the team.

Scripture says to rejoice with those who rejoice and to weep with those who weep (Romans 12:15). That's what a team does. We win together, and we lose together. Although that one star forward scored the winning goal in overtime, what would have happened if one of your players on the bench had not yelled out to your backside full-back that number 10 was making a run in behind him unmarked? That piece of information yelled out by one of your bench players that prevented a goal was just as important to the outcome of the game as the score by your player on the field.

THOUGHTS TO PONDER:

- What other things can I do to recognize my nonstarters?
- Describe the impact you expect to see once you start to positively recognize all of your team members in some way.

ATTITUDE TOWARD
YOUR PLAYERS

But because of his great love for us, God, who is rich in mercy, made us alive
with Christ even when we were dead in transgressions—it is by grace you have
been saved. And God raised us up with Christ and seated us with him in the heav-
enly realms in Christ Jesus, in order that in the coming ages he might show the
incomparable riches of his grace, expressed in his kindness to us in Christ Jesus.
—EPHESIANS 2:4–7, NIV

MAGINE THIS: You are in the presence of a very powerful ruler. He
motions for you to come and stand before him. You are thinking,
Who, me? But you know he is looking straight at you. You cautiously
proceed with fear and trembling, wondering, *What in the world does
he want with me?* With legs shaking and knees about to cave in, you
make your way to the appointed spot. He rises majestically from his
throne and reaches to grab something shiny on the table beside him.
He tells you to cup your hands together in front of yourself. Once you
do, he places the shiny object in your hands. You look down at it, and
it is a precious jewel, glittering in the light. You ask the ruler, "What
is this?" He says, "This precious gemstone represents the souls of the
players I give you to coach." At that, you awaken from the dream,
sit up in bed, and notice that your heart is beating fast and you are
breathing heavy.

As a Christian who (also) happens to be a coach, you must realize
that you are called to purpose. Your life is not just willy-nilly and hap-
hazard. You are placed in situations to fulfill a God-given purpose.
Sometimes you get to see that purpose fulfilled from start to finish,
and other times you are there only for a short time. Either way, your
mission is to do and to be what God has purposed for you for the

situation. The players you are privileged to coach are sent to you for a reason. You are to see them as jewels, precious jewels, from the hand of God. You are to influence them, teach them, encourage them, and train them. The soccer part is an added bonus.

I love seeing one of my former players or talking on the phone with them. It is not uncommon for me to see a former player who says something like "So good to see you,

> The players you are privileged to coach are sent to you for a reason.

Coach! Coach, I just want to thank you for teaching me about life. I didn't always want to hear what you had to say back then, but many times through the years I have remembered your words to me. Now I realize how true they were, and I just want you to know that I appreciate you so much." Needless to say, at that point I am very humbled and pretty much puddlelized. (That's my word.)

The only thing better than that is when they tell me they have given their life to the Lord and are following Him as a Christian.

THOUGHTS TO PONDER:

- Do I see my players as gifts from God to me?
- If so, how does this affect the way I relate to and handle them? If not, how would a shift in perspective help me and my team?

COLLABORATE WITH ADMINISTRATION

Whatever you do, work at it with all your heart, as working for the Lord, not for human masters, since you know that you will receive an inheritance from the Lord as a reward. It is the Lord Christ you are serving.
—COLOSSIANS 3:23–24, NIV

A s I MENTIONED in an earlier day's devotional, having supportive leadership is vitally important to a coach, as it makes his or her efforts more productive. Every national team coach has a governing body or federation overseeing him or her. Every professional coach has an owner and management team looking over the coach's shoulders. For every college coach, there is an athletic director and some type of college board that supervises the coach or coaches. In high school sports, there is usually an athletic director and a principal, plus a district governing board, in charge. For club and recreation teams, there is an association that watches over everyone. The people who oversee you as coach can encourage you and build you and your program up—or they can wear you down.

> Support and encouragement should flow both ways, from the administration to the coach and from the coach to the administration.

If you are an administrator who helps oversee a coach or coaches, look for ways to be helpful to that coach and program. If you have a quality coach, I can promise you that he or she is not only putting together the strategies and x's and o's of the game, but also acting as a counselor, mother, father, and instructor to help the players develop as people. Whatever support you can give to that coach will only improve the quality of the product both on and off the field.

If you are a coach, I humbly request you let your requests be made known unto God and your supervisors. They may not be able to grant every single request you have, but work with them as they work with you. There's only so much money to go around, and there are only so many bodies available to help. Support and encouragement should flow both ways, from the administration to the coach and from the coach to the administration. By working together, everyone is more likely to accomplish their goals.

THOUGHTS TO PONDER:

- Far too often, coaches and management are at odds with each other rather than working together. As a coach, what are some ways you can work to improve the relationship you have with management?

- The scripture above says to do your work unto the Lord because He is our ultimate master and the One that you serve. If you apply that scripture to your job as soccer coach, how does it affect or change the way you perform your coaching duties?

- How does that scripture affect the way I relate to those who oversee me?

WIN WITH GRACE

But he gives us more grace. That is why Scripture says: "God
opposes the proud but shows favor to the humble."
—JAMES 4:6, NIV

"For those who make themselves great will be humbled, and
those who humble themselves will be made great."
—LUKE 14:11, GNT

WINNING IS A wonderful thing! Personally, I don't know of anyone who would rather lose than win. Most of us have a competitive nature, and we want to win. Winning puts us on top (whatever "top" is). Winning brings us fame. Winning makes us feel good. Winning makes other people feel good about us. Winning elevates us in people's eyes.

But there are questions to ask about winning. Here are two of them:

1. Do we win at all costs?

2. How do we behave when we win?

Let's look at the first question. Do we win at all costs? As Christians who are followers of Christ, absolutely not. We do not cheat in order to win. We do not intentionally hurt our opponents in order to win. We do not break the rules for the sake of winning. Our conduct must model the integrity of Christ.

Now let's look at the second question. How do we behave when we win? We win with grace. We are grateful when we win. Remember, gratefulness automatically carries an attitude of humility with it. Do we celebrate? Absolutely! Yes! But we celebrate with joy, not by being arrogant. We celebrate with appreciation for the hard work we put into the game to get the win, not by looking down on those who lost. We celebrate by recognizing the parents and fans, our teammates, those who did not get to play, and the referees. We give credit to whom credit is due,

> Many life lessons can be learned from winning, especially winning the right way.

so we shake hands with the opposing team and acknowledge the hustle and talent they displayed on the field also.

Many life lessons can be learned from winning, especially winning the right way. The primary lesson is that even though we hustled our tails off to get the win, we did not win by ourselves. It took the help and cooperation of the teammates and the coaches along with the support of medical staff, administration, parents, fans, and sponsors to bring it all together for the win. In life, we work hard to position ourselves for better living, but still others come alongside us to help us and encourage us in some way that propels us along.

No matter what you do, win with grace by having an attitude of gratefulness and humility.

THOUGHTS TO PONDER:

- Who are people I need to acknowledge for helping me be successful?
- Describe the difference between winning with grace and winning with arrogance.

LOSE WITH GRACE

Let us not become weary in doing good, for at the proper time we will reap a harvest if we do not give up.
—GALATIANS 6:9, NIV

OSING STINKS, PURE and simple. I am a fairly mild-mannered, even-tempered guy. But I hate losing. My competitive nature kicks in when it's game time. Not that I was ever a great athlete, but I do have a competitive nature about me. When my two children were living at home, even through their early teen and college years, the two of them and my wife hated playing Monopoly with me because I was cutthroat and would take everything I could buy. They would then have to pay me enormous rents and go broke. I loved it. They hated it and eventually refused to play me anymore. We haven't played since then. So I know I was not winning gracefully—but that was family.

During my first two years of coaching, we lost more games than we won. We lost some close games, and we were on the losing end of some blowouts. Both can be tough to handle. For the close-game losses, you feel like, *If we had just done this or done that, we could have won that game.* So you feel bad about that. For the blowout losses, you feel hopeless because your team was just not able to compete equally with the other team. So you feel bad about that as well.

How do you lose with grace? You lose with grace by turning the loss into a winning, teachable moment and by finding hope to build upon. You also handle the loss gracefully.

In those early years of losing, I learned a lot about coaching. I would evaluate what our opportunities for improvement were from previous games, and I would determine how we could keep improving on that aspect of the game. Then in our next practices, we would work on those skills, and I would be sure to mention to the players that they were improving in those areas. This would give them confidence they didn't have before. Confidence is contagious. It spreads throughout the team.

> You lose with grace by turning the loss into a winning, teachable moment and by finding hope to build upon.

I would also emphasize displaying good sportsmanship to my players, whether the other team did or not. We may have lost the game, but we were not going to lose in sportsmanship. I also made it my business to complement players from the other team who were very talented and played in a commendable way. My players would see me talking with an opposing player, and they knew what I was doing. This was sending a message to them without telling them the message. Even though losing is not fun, you can lose with dignity and class, and you can turn the loss into a positive if you handle it correctly.

THOUGHTS TO PONDER:

- What are some specific ways I can turn a loss into a positive experience for me and my team?

- In relation to the scripture above from Galatians 6:9, what "doing good" are you involved in, and when will you see the harvest from your investment?

DEALING WITH A DIFFICULT PLAYER

Religion that God our Father accepts as pure and faultless is this: to look after orphans and widows in their distress and to keep oneself from being polluted by the world.
—JAMES 1:27, NIV

"Then the King will say to the people on his right, 'Come, you that are blessed by my Father! Come and possess the kingdom which has been prepared for you ever since the creation of the world. I was hungry and you fed me, thirsty and you gave me a drink; I was a stranger and you received me in your homes, naked and you clothed me; I was sick and you took care of me, in prison and you visited me.' The righteous will then answer him, 'When, Lord, did we ever see you hungry and feed you, or thirsty and give you a drink? When did we ever see you a stranger and welcome you in our homes, or naked and clothe you? When did we ever see you sick or in prison, and visit you?' The King will reply, 'I tell you, whenever you did this for one of the least important of these followers of mine, you did it for me!'"
—MATTHEW 25:34–40, GNT

EVERY NOW AND then in life, you get handed a bag of lemons. It becomes your job to take those sour lemons and make sweet, delicious lemonade. How do you do that? You roll them gently back and forth with the palms of your hands. You squeeze them until you feel each lemon getting tender on the inside. You cut them and squeeze out the lemon juice into a container. You add in water and something to turn the sour into sweet, such as sugar. You mix all of that up real good, and voilà! You've got lemonade.

As a soccer coach, or even as a player sometimes, you might receive a gift of a new player to your team that is a little more difficult to handle than most of your other players. How you handle that person is critical and can affect their life for good or bad for years to come. But your actions, reactions, and attitude toward this player also send a message to the rest of the team. They will take their lead from you and your example, and respond accordingly.

One thing I have learned is that you never know what type of home life or background a player is coming from or what is going on in a player's life at the moment. A player who is exhibiting antisocial behavior may very well be crying out to be loved and accepted. When she pulls away from the others, what she really wants is for someone to come over to her, be with her, and listen. When a player exhibits anger and has a verbal outburst, it may be because he sees the other players' parents at the game but has no parent there to support and cheer for him.

> The important thing to remember is to pray for this player (as well as all of your players) and to seek God's guidance for what to do.

The important thing to remember is to pray for this player (as well as all of your players) and to seek God's guidance for what to do. Look for the right opportunity to pull them aside, and let them know in an appropriate way that you care about them and are available to listen and help if you can. Your genuineness will make a world of difference to them. Their world probably won't get all better overnight, but just knowing someone sincerely cares will truly matter to them.

Thoughts to ponder:

- What gift (player) has the Lord brought across my path that I totally mishandled?

- What can I do going forward when I'm dealing with a player who is going through a rough time?

- In light of the two scriptures listed above, what should be my response and attitude toward players who are experiencing a difficult time?

PARENTS: SUPPORT YOUR PLAYER'S COACH

"Why, then, do you look at the speck in your brother's eye and pay no attention to the log in your own eye? How dare you say to your brother, 'Please, let me take that speck out of your eye,' when you have a log in your own eye? You hypocrite! First take the log out of your own eye, and then you will be able to see clearly to take the speck out of your brother's eye."

—Matthew 7:3–5, GNT

First of all, then, I urge that petitions, prayers, requests, and thanksgivings be offered to God for all people; for kings and all others who are in authority, that we may live a quiet and peaceful life with all reverence toward God and with proper conduct. This is good and it pleases God our Savior.
—1 Timothy 2:1–3, GNT

"Blessed are the peacemakers, for they will be called children of God."
—Matthew 5:9, NIV

I'LL ADMIT IT: I'm old fashioned. When I was a teenager, I thought my parents had just about lost it and were simply not "with it" in the modern world of that time. Then, about five years later, I got married, started having children of my own, and realized that my parents were not so bad after all. When I reached my thirties, it hit me that my parents were and had been absolute geniuses. I share this because when I was in school and living under my parents' roof and authority, they always took the side of the teacher and supported the teacher if there was an issue at school, at least initially. It wasn't that they thought I was automatically wrong, but they wanted to hear the teacher's perspective before taking my side of the situation. I appreciate that today.

In today's world, way too many times it is the exact opposite. If there is a problem between a player and coach, lots of parents today instantly side with their child and the coach is presumed to be at fault. This causes further issues on the team and raises tension and stress. I have seen far too many parents yell and scream at their child's coach and blame the coach for every problem. Some parents seem to think their child can do no wrong. They know better than that, but in public they can't admit to it because they think it reflects on them.

> Speak well of the coach to others, and look for ways to support what the coach wants for the team.

Parents, please support your player's coaches. No coach is perfect, and no coach will do everything right. But remember that you've got someone who is taking the time to invest in—as well as mentor, teach, encourage, and train—your child and others. When there are issues that need to be addressed, find an appropriate time and place to speak with the coach, and do so in a respectful manner. Then listen as objectively as you can and work together to make things better. Speak well of the coach to others, and look for ways to support what the coach wants for the team. If you genuinely have a rotten apple for a coach, then take it to the proper authorities and let them deal with it. Spreading poison only makes the matter worse.

THOUGHTS TO PONDER:

- When there is strife within my team, what are ways I can be a peacemaker?

- Although your child's coach may not be your favorite coach or person, think about and list some advantages of supporting him or her instead of tearing them down.

- Of the three scriptures listed above, which one speaks to me the strongest, and why?

COACH: SUPPORT YOUR PLAYERS' PARENTS

*Children, obey your parents in the Lord, for this is right. "Honor your father
and mother"—which is the first commandment with a promise—"so that it
may go well with you and that you may enjoy long life on the earth."*
—EPHESIANS 6:1–3, NIV

*My child, pay attention to what your father and mother tell
you. Their teaching will improve your character as a hand-
some turban or a necklace improves your appearance.*
—PROVERBS 1:8, 9, GNT

"Blessed are the peacemakers, for they will be called children of God."
—MATTHEW 5:9, NIV

W E START THIS devotion with three quotes. The first is from
Billy Graham: "A coach will impact more young people in
a year than the average person does in a lifetime." Here
is another quote, but I don't know who the author is: "A coach can
influence an athlete more than any other person, except possibly the
parents." The last quote is from John Wooden: "A coach is someone
who can give correction without causing resentment." Wow! Parents
wish they had that secret weapon.

Coaches, you need to realize the sway you have over your players.
Because they are a part of your team, they want to please you, so they
will listen to you. They will go the extra mile for you. They will do
what you say (for the most part). They are heavily influenced by you.
Because of that, you also have the power to positively impact the relationship between a player and his or her parent(s). This is especially

relevant if you are coaching teenagers. Teens are at the stage in life where they are questioning and doubting their parents. They want more freedom than the parents are giving, and they think they are fully grown now and should be able to make all of their own decisions. Many times, for this age group, there

> Be a bridge builder and a peacemaker when you have the opportunity.

is strife in the home because of the tension going on between them and their parent(s). You, as a coach, can help.

"How can I help?" you ask. Sometimes a player or a parent, or both, will come to you to tell you about a situation and ask for your opinion about what should be done. Other times you will sense that something is not right between a player and their parent(s), and you'll become more intentionally observant and prayerful. Whenever you have these types of conversations with a player or when you are giving a "life-lesson sermon" to your team, throw in a nugget that supports their parents. Mention that their parents love them and only want the best for them. Encourage them to share their thoughts and feelings with their parents in a respectful way. Let them know that parents are not perfect people but that they have the best interest of their children at heart. Be a bridge builder and a peacemaker when you have the opportunity. You will be blessed for it.

THOUGHTS TO PONDER:

- In thinking about some of the not-so-good player/parent relationships you've seen, what are some ways you can work to be a bridge builder and a peacemaker?

- Reread the three quotes listed in the first paragraph. Write out your thoughts and reactions to them.

BUILD YOUR TEAM'S CULTURE

Commit to the LORD whatever you do, and he will establish your plans.
—PROVERBS 16:3, NIV

Unless the LORD builds the house, the builders labor in vain.
—PSALM 127:1, NIV

The plans of the diligent lead to profit as surely as haste leads to poverty.
—PROVERBS 21:5, NIV

WINNING TEAMS HAVE a culture. What is the culture of your team? In the very early years of my coaching career, I didn't really think about developing a team culture. I was too busy learning the game and figuring out the best strategies to use for the players I had. What I didn't realize was that culture was being developed without my intentionally working at it.

You might wonder, *What is team culture?* Different people will likely answer this in varying ways, but for me, team culture is a mix of established traditions, expectations and standards, attitude, and ethics and values that are established and upheld over time. One consistent aspect of my team culture through the years was having fun. It seemed that every year, we had one, if not two, players who were straight-up comedians and could keep me and the team laughing throughout the season. I believe that helped us to play loose and with creativity on the field. We worked really hard during preseason, but we had lots of fun during the regular season.

Another part of my team culture was that I listened to them and their ideas. I made it known each year that I was the head coach, but I respected their ideas and opinions as well, and I wanted to hear them. I told them I would always give consideration to their suggestions but that the final decision would be mine. Believe me, I received some very good ideas from my players through the years, and I implemented most of them. Those that I didn't implement, I had a very good reason for not doing so. By giving my players freedom to give me feedback and by showing them I would listen to them, I gave them the freedom to make adjustments on the fly during a game. This usually worked out well, but the few times I didn't like what they did, I would simply tell them what I wanted them to do, and they would do it.

> Your team culture will be an invisible guide and a parameter for your team's success.

Your team culture will be an invisible guide and a parameter for your team's success. Give thought to what values your team upholds every year. What are the team standards and expectations? What are the established traditions? Also, what is the overall attitude or climate within your team? All of these are integral to your team culture and the success your team will have year in and year out.

THOUGHTS TO PONDER:

- Take some time to answer the questions in the last paragraph.

- Having answered those questions, what are some changes I want to implement or get rid of?

- In light of the three scriptures listed above, what should I do with the plans I have for my team?

IS SOCCER YOUR GOD?

"You shall have no other gods before me."
—EXODUS 20:3, NIV

Jesus answered, "It is written: 'Worship the Lord your God and serve him only.'"
—LUKE 4:8, NIV

SOCCER IS KNOWN the world over as "the beautiful game," and what a fitting title. When soccer is played correctly, with high-quality players and teams, it is a beautiful game to watch, with lots of ooh's and aah's mixed in. But soccer can also be very addictive. As a matter of fact, there are lots of addictions we have to deal with in life. Some include food and sports addictions, as well as emotional, chemical, and physical addictions.

When we are addicted to something, we serve it. We give a lot of time to it, and we spend a lot of our time with it. We feel lost and out of place without it. We have to be exposed to it or partake of it again after not too long. We taste it. We feed it. We live it. We breathe it.

I know a lot of people who would not admit it publicly, but, truthfully, soccer is their god. I, too, had to do a self-check years ago on how much the game was controlling my life. I had to place

> When we are addicted to something, we serve it.

parameters around my soccer exposure; I decided to significantly reduce the amount of time I spent watching soccer and working on soccer-related coaching duties. This decision benefitted my relationship with my wife and my personal health.

If you are willing to honestly evaluate the place soccer holds in your life, you might find out that soccer is an idol for you. How much money do you put into the game? How much time do you spend playing it, practicing for it, coaching it, watching it, researching it, and talking about it? Now compare that to the amount of time you spend communing with God, reading His word, worshipping Him, and fellowshipping with His people. Which one comes out with receiving the most of your energy, time, passion, and resources?

THOUGHTS TO PONDER:

- I've given you much to consider and think about already in today's devotion. So your assignment is to read back through it and slowly work your way through the questions and thoughts I have shared in this lesson. Be honest with yourself and God, and listen to what He tells you.

- Remember, there is no condemnation in Christ (Romans 8:1), but God does convict us of wrongdoing by His Spirit. If repentance is needed, offer it, and then get up and rejoice in the Lord.

THE BALANCING ACT

*"But seek first his kingdom and his righteousness, and all
these things will be given to you as well."*
—MATTHEW 6:33, NIV

L ET'S CREATE AN imaginary person who is a soccer coach. We will name her Diedre. She is thirty-five years old, married, with two girls, ages ten and eight. She played college soccer and is currently coaching high school girls. Diedre is also active in the women's ministry at her church and teaches at the school. Her parents live two hours away, and her dad is not in the best of health. Her husband, Marty, is a CPA (certified public accountant) in town.

Without receiving any further details, do you see any challenges Diedre and Marty might have? What are some challenges Diedre probably has?

Overall, there are a number of challenges and tasks Diedre must handle on a consistent basis. She needs to find some type of proper balance in her life and schedule.

First, she is a Christian who is committed to the Lord. She is a wife and mother. She is an adult daughter. She is an active participant in her church family. She is a high school girls' soccer coach. As Diedre looks to prioritize items in her life, will she find that what she prioritizes as first takes up the most time in her life? Probably not. It usually doesn't work out that way.

To figure this out, Diedre has decided that her personal time with the Lord will be her number one priority. She has determined to spend daily time early each morning in devotion and communion with the Lord. She has also decided that she and Marty need time together every evening after the children go to bed, just to catch up with each other and listen and share heart-to-heart conversation with one another. She will call and check on her dad at least every other day and go visit on the weekends as needed.

Although she really enjoys being part of the women's ministry at church, she has decided to step back from helping lead the spring pantry drive but will help support it. She already made the decision to not play in the adult coed soccer league this fall, but she did join the local fitness center for the purpose of improving her physical fitness. She has also decided to limit the time her soccer girls can call or come by her house so she can give more time to her own girls.

> Regardless of whether this scene fits your life or not, you need to figure out your life priorities and adjust your schedule as needed.

Does any of this sound familiar to you or anyone you know? I have found this scenario to be quite representative of many soccer coaches' lives. Regardless of whether this scene fits your life or not, you need to figure out your life priorities and adjust your schedule as needed.

THOUGHTS TO PONDER:

- What are my set priorities? List them out in numerical order.

- Write down what you think it means to seek first the kingdom of God and His righteousness and how this applies to your life.

STUDENT FIRST, ATHLETE SECOND

So whether you eat or drink or whatever you do, do it all for the glory of God.
—1 Corinthians 10:31, niv

*Whatever you do, work at it with all your heart, as though
you were working for the Lord and not for people.*
—Colossians 3:23, gnt

HERE IS A common conversation, one I have had numerous times through the years with various soccer players. I start by asking, "So, what are your plans for when you finish high school?"

The player's typical response is, "I hope to go pro and play for a professional team."

"You do realize you have to be the best of the best to get to that level," I say, "and very few people get there?"

Then they say, "Coach, do you not think I'm good enough to play in the pros?"

The passion many of my players through the years had for soccer was unmatched when it came to the typical basketball, football, or baseball player, from what I saw. Soccer was their life and their strong passion, and they dreamed of being the next Messi or Ronaldo since they were a little child. I never tried to crush the hopes and dreams of my players, but I did try to get them to face reality and see that they probably should have a plan B, just in case plan A didn't work out for them.

Even for college and professional athletes who make it big, serious injuries and concussions can bring their athletic career to an abrupt and permanent end. When this happens, their plans have to change suddenly, and they must pursue a new career path.

If you are a student athlete, I highly encourage you to do your best in school. Don't miss out on an award or scholarship because your grade point average was one-tenth of a point too low (like mine was)

> Your grades and your behavior will open doors for you and close doors for you.

and if you had just applied yourself even a little bit more, you could have covered that gap with no problem at all.

Your grades and your behavior will open doors for you and close doors for you. Don't leave a part of your life, only to look back with regret, knowing you could have done much better if you had just applied yourself to your studies more. Be ready to take advantage of the many opportunities that lay before you. Enjoy school, but also use it for the main purposes it is designed for.

THOUGHTS TO PONDER:

- Why has God created me? What is my mission in life?
- (If you need help figuring this out and don't have anyone locally to help you, send me an email at kmsham41@gmail.com, and I will be happy to assist you.)
- In what area of my academics could I give better effort?
- (If you are genuinely struggling and need help academically, don't be too proud to ask for help. Talk with a parent or guardian, school counselor, teacher, or someone you know who has your best interest at heart, and get the help you need.)

PRAYER TO BECOME A FOLLOWER OF JESUS CHRIST

THIS BOOK WAS written to and for Christians who also love the game of soccer. However, after writing the devotionals, I realized that everyone who reads this may not be a dedicated follower of Christ. So, if you want to give your life to the Lord Jesus, or if you followed Christ at one time but have since strayed away from Him, allow me the privilege to lead you back to Him by praying this prayer with utmost sincerity:

Father God, thank You for loving me unconditionally. Your love is drawing me to You, and I choose You this day. Please forgive me of my many sins and for living life my own way. Thank You, Lord, for saving me and for forgiving me. Thank You for cleansing me and for making me a brand-new creation in Christ Jesus. I choose Jesus as my Lord and Savior right now, and I ask You, Lord, to fill me with Your Holy Spirit to empower me to live a victorious Christian life. Thank You, Lord, for Your goodness to me, and thank You for accepting me into Your family. Amen!

Welcome, my brother or sister, to the family of God! Just like a newborn baby needs to be fed, nurtured, and taken care of, likewise you, as a new believer in Christ, need similar spiritual food and nourishment. I strongly encourage you to make your next steps the following:

- Start reading God's Word, the Bible (preferably the book of John in the New Testament), and take time to pray to the Lord every day.

- Find a quality Christian church or fellowship, if you are not part of one already. Find one where the Word of God is preached boldly and where the people have a genuine heart to pursue God and love others.

- Get water baptized.

If you need help with any of this, feel free to contact me at masterpiececs19@gmail.com.

by Dr. Cynthia Thrasher Shamberger

SUCCESS AS A SOCCER MOM

"There is a lad here who has five barley loaves and two
small fish, but what are they among so many?"
—JOHN 6:9, NKJV

Jesus replied, "They do not need to go away.
You give them something to eat."
"We have here only five loaves of bread and two fish," they answered. "Bring
them here to me," he said. And he directed the people to sit down on the
grass. Taking the five loaves and the two fish and looking up to heaven, he gave
thanks and broke the loaves. Then he gave them to the disciples, and the dis-
ciples gave them to the people. They all ate and were satisfied, and the disciples
picked up twelve basketfuls of broken pieces that were left over. The number of
those who ate was about five thousand men, besides women and children.
—MATTHEW 14:16–21, NIV

Packing lunch. What a seemingly mundane task. Often it's the same boring lunch that's been packed many times before. Sometimes it may be wonderful leftovers from a special occasion. At other times, you may wonder if there will be anything to pack for lunch at all. Yes, preparing lunch can be a challenge, and it is usually a thankless job.

But as soccer moms, fathers, siblings, or other family and friends who find ourselves in the position to influence our soccer player (no matter the age or level), we should follow the example of the nameless mom or other caregiver who not only prepared a lunch of fish and bread but also prepared the heart of a boy to seek after Jesus. The boy recognized the reality of what he possessed (and so did the disciples). Yet in the face of the hungry, onlooking crowd, he was willing to offer his small lunch to Jesus. In the hands of the Master, what was prepared in obscurity was blessed and multiplied—and we're still excited about the results today. What will our soccer player do with his gifts and talents . . . or lack thereof?

How do we relate to our player on and off the field? In private and in public? How do we react to the thrill of victory and the agony of defeat—or no playing time at all?

> We must model what we desire to pour into the lives of others.

We must model what we desire to pour into the lives of others. Jesus's perspective of who we are, what we have, and what we can accomplish is much higher than ours. His way of doing things is far beyond our way. We must make a priority of seeking to be in the Lord's presence all through the day every day. We must resist crowd-pleasing and submit to the crowd-feeding Soul Freer—Jesus! Let's rethink our ordinary, everyday lives as soccer moms. Let's prepare our hearts and the hearts of our children to obey God's Word and to serve the Lord with all that we have and all that we are. May our lives on and off the field be a legacy to the wonderful glory of God!

Thoughts to ponder:

- Write a sentence or two about an area of your life that seems boring and insignificant. Ask the Lord to give you fresh vision by showing you His perspective.

- Ask the Lord to show you scripture to meditate on concerning how He sees you and your abilities.

- Say a short prayer to the Lord, thanking Him in the face of—and asking Him for help with—the small, boring chores and the overwhelming, impossible-looking tasks. Begin to do this often, and watch God work!

WIN AS A SOCCER WIFE

For the entire law is fulfilled in keeping this one com-
mand: "Love your neighbor as yourself."
—GALATIANS 5:14, NIV

Submit yourselves, then, to God. Resist the devil, and he will flee
from you. Come near to God and he will come near to you.
—JAMES 4:7–8, NIV

She is clothed with strength and dignity; she can laugh at the days to come.
—PROVERBS 31:25, NIV

Let the morning bring me word of your unfailing love, for I have put my
trust in you. Show me the way I should go, for to you I entrust my life.
– PSALM 143.8

LONELY, RESENTFUL, AND jealous are some of the feelings I experienced at times during nearly twenty years as a "soccer wife." Early in my husband's coaching career, the team affectionately called me Mrs. Coach, which I enjoyed. However, as the program developed, I felt soccer was getting more of my husband's energy and attention than I was. The low salary and long hours away from home; constantly hearing about the problems, issues, and even triumphs of coaching while trying to be supportive yet wanting more attention for myself and our household—these things were frustrating year after year.

Desperate to end my toxic thoughts and negative attitude toward soccer, I started telling God how I felt, asking Him to help me, my husband, and our marriage. I began to pray more strategically regarding soccer. I gained strength, wisdom, and comfort from God's Word and from spending time in His presence. As a result, I slowly realized that even if I was right in my assessment of the situation, my response to it was wrong. Sure, we are created to experience emotions, but as new creations in Christ, we are to let the Word of God rule us instead of our emotions.

Empowered and encouraged by God's Word, I began to pray more specifically for and with my husband-coach and for the boys whose lives he was helping to shape. I embraced his coaching as ministry ordained by God and realized he had to answer to God for our marriage and coaching too. When the reality of being a soccer wife would show up again as fear on a lonely, rainy, away-game night or in the anxiety of tournament season, I would focus on God and His Word. For example, I remembered with gratitude that my husband supported me through two graduate degrees, which involved long hours away from him and a strain on our budget.

> I gained strength, wisdom, and comfort from God's Word and from spending time in His presence.

Another example is that I began to walk when I attended games. I was supporting my husband and the team by attending and praying for both teams, and I was getting in much-needed exercise while singing praises to God. This was definitely a win-win situation. The Lord is always faithful. I don't have all of the answers. I don't know why I had to be a soccer wife. But I have come to know the peace of God in a greater way, and He has helped me win over my thoughts, emotions, and circumstances.

THOUGHTS TO PONDER:

- Forgive your spouse, and ask the Lord to forgive you so your prayers are not hindered.

- Write a note to God that lists things you are thankful for regarding soccer.

- Make a list of things you don't like about how soccer affects your marriage or other important relationships (maybe your parent or sibling is in soccer and you are not). Then date it and pray over the list often. Remember to thank God and add answers to prayer, along with dates, as they occur.

IF YOU'RE A FAN OF THIS BOOK, WILL YOU HELP ME SPREAD THE WORD?

There are several ways you can help me get the word out about the message of this book...

- Post a 5-Star review on Amazon.
- Write about the book on your Facebook, Twitter, Instagram, LinkedIn, – any social media you regularly use!
- If you blog, consider referencing the book, or publishing an excerpt from the book with a link back to my website. You have my permission to do this as long as you provide proper credit and backlinks.
- Recommend the book to friends – word-of-mouth is still the most effective form of advertising.
- Purchase additional copies to give away as gifts.

The best way to connect with me is by:
masterpiececs19@gmail.com or
visit my website masterpiececs.com

NEED A DYNAMIC SPEAKER FOR YOUR NEXT EVENT?

HOW ABOUT COACHING YOUR GROUP TO THE NEXT LEVEL OF SUCCESS?

As president and founder of Masterpiece Consulting Solutions, LLC., I offer consulting services to individuals, churches, teams and organizations to help them move past roadblocks and achieve new heights of success.

I offer workshops in:

- Leadership Development
- Improving Communication Skills
- Time Management
- Finding Your Place in Ministry
- and more.

I will customize my services to fit the specific needs of those I am serving. I am available for speaking engagements–keynote addresses, motivational workshops and more.

Contact me at: masterpiececs19@gmail.com or visit my website masterpiececs.com